Autumn

by Gail Saunders-Smith

Content Consultant:
Lisa M. Nyberg, Ph.D.
Educator, Springfield (Oregon) Public Schools

Pebble Books

an imprint of Capstone Press

Pebble Books

Pebble Books are published by Capstone Press
818 North Willow Street, Mankato, Minnesota 56001
http://www.capstone-press.com

Library of Congress Cataloging-in-Publication Data
Saunders-Smith, Gail.
    Autumn/by Gail Saunders-Smith.
        p. cm.
    Includes bibliographical references and index.
    Summary: Simple text and photographs depict the weather, plants, animals, and activities of
autumn.
    ISBN 1-56065-783-9
    1. Autumn—Juvenile literature. [1. Autumn.] I. Title.
    QB637.7.S28 1998
    508.2—dc21   98-5042
                                                                  CIP
                                                                  AC

Note to Parents and Teachers

This book describes and illustrates the changes in weather, people, plants, and
animals in autumn. The close picture-text matches support early readers in
understanding the text. The text offers subtle challenges with compound and
complex sentence structures. This book also introduces early readers to
expository and content-specific vocabulary. The expository vocabulary is
defined in the Words to Know section. Early readers may need assistance in
reading some of these words. Readers also may need assistance in using the
Table of Contents, Words to Know, Read More, Internet Sites, and Index/Word
List sections of the book.

2

Table of Contents

4

Autumn is a season for preparing for winter. Autumn comes after summer and before winter. Another name for autumn is fall.

Days can still be warm during autumn. But days turn cooler as it gets close to winter. Sometimes there is frost on the ground.

Many students go back to school in autumn. People also play sports. Some people play football and soccer.

People rake leaves that fall from trees. They prepare their homes for winter. They bring out warm clothes.

Some leaves change color during autumn. The leaves stop making chlorophyll. Chlorophyll is what makes leaves look green. Other colors show through when chlorophyll is not in the leaves. Leaves turn red, yellow, orange, or brown.

Some fruits and vegetables ripen during autumn. People pick pumpkins, apples, and potatoes. Farmers harvest corn and wheat.

Some animals eat more during autumn. Bears eat more to build up fat in their bodies. Bears hibernate during winter. Hibernate is to sleep deeply. Bears do not eat much while they hibernate. Bears use the fat in their bodies for food in the winter.

Squirrels hide food in autumn. They save it for winter. Many animals grow heavy winter coats. They find warm places to stay.

Some birds, butterflies, and whales migrate in autumn. They go to warmer places for winter. Autumn is a season for getting ready for winter.

Words to Know

chlorophyll—food for the plant; something that makes leaves a green color

corn—a green plant that makes yellow or white seeds; people and animals eat the seeds

frost—very small pieces of ice that cover grass and trees when the weather turns cold

hibernate—to sleep deeply through winter

migrate—to move to another place to live for a season

potato—a thick root of a plant that people eat

season—one of the four parts of a year; spring, summer, autumn, and winter

student—a person who goes to school

wheat—a type of grass whose seed is used to make bread and other foods

Read More

Gibbons, Gail. *The Reasons for Seasons.* New York: Holiday House, 1995.

Maestro, Betsy. *Why Do Leaves Change Color?* New York: HarperCollins, 1994.

Saunders-Smith, Gail. *Animals in the Fall.* Mankato, Minn.: Pebble Books, 1998.

Internet Sites

4 Seasons: Fall
http://www.rescol.ca/collections/agriculture/fall.html

Meaning of "Fall"/Identifying the Changing Leaves
http://www.mobot.org/MBGnet/fr/temp/color.htm

Signs of the Seasons
http://www.4seasons.org.uk/projects/seasons/index.html

Index/Word List

Word Count: 224
Early-Intervention, 11

Editorial Credits

Lois Wallentine, editor; Timothy Halldin, design; Michelle L. Norstad, photo research

Photo Credits

Jean S. Buldain, 1
Cheryl A. Ertlet, 6
GeoImagery/Jan W. Jorolan, 12
Dwight Kuhn, 18
William Munoz, 16
James P. Rowan, 20
Kay Shaw, 4
Unicorn Stock Photos/Joel Dexter, cover; Ron Holt, 8; Alice M. Prescott, 10; Jeff Greenberg, 14